MW01173007

THIS

*Journal*

BELONGS TO:

DATE:

Made in the USA
Columbia, SC
04 February 2023

11749533R00067